My Feelings Journal

_____

_____

Date ....
Today I mostly feel....... (Circle One)

Or Draw your own emoji!

How Have You Been Feeling?

I am mad and sad because
my mum wouldn't let me play

Something That Helped You Today:

_____

_____

_____

3 Good Things about today:

① _____

② _____

③ _____

Write/Draw/Doodle About Your Day!

Write About Your Day Or Anything You Want!

_____

_____

_____

Goals or Aims For Tomorrow?

_____

_____

_____

Date ....

Today I mostly feel....... (Circle One)

😀	😊	😐	🙁	😢	😠

Or Draw ◯ your own emoji!

How Have You Been Feeling?

_____

_____

_____

Something That Helped You Today:

_____

_____

_____

3 Good Things about today:

① _____

② _____

③ _____

Write/Draw/Doodle About Your Day!

Write About Your Day Or Anything You Want!

_____

_____

_____

Goals or Aims For Tomorrow?

_____

_____

_____

Date ....

Today I mostly feel......... (Circle One)

Or Draw ⟶ ◯ your own emoji!

How Have You Been Feeling?

_____

_____

_____

Something That Helped You Today:

_____

_____

_____

3 Good Things about today:

① _____

② _____

③ _____

Write/Draw/Doodle About Your Day!

Write About Your Day Or Anything You Want!

_____

_____

_____

Goals or Aims For Tomorrow?

_____

_____

_____

Date ....
Today I mostly feel........ (Circle One)

Or Draw ( ) your own emoji!

How Have You Been Feeling?
_____
_____
_____

Something That Helped You Today:

_____

_____

_____

3 Good Things about today:
① _____
② _____
③ _____

Write/Draw/Doodle About Your Day!

Write About Your Day Or Anything You Want!

_____

_____

_____

Goals or Aims For Tomorrow?

_____

_____

_____

Date ....

Today I mostly feel........ (Circle One)

Or Draw your own emoji!

How Have You Been Feeling?

_____

_____

_____

Something That Helped You Today:

_____

_____

_____

3 Good Things about today:

① _____

② _____

③ _____

Write/Draw/Doodle About Your Day!

Write About Your Day Or Anything You Want!

_____

_____

_____

Goals or Aims For Tomorrow?

_____

_____

_____

Date ....

Today I mostly feel...... (Circle One)

How Have You Been Feeling?

_____

_____

_____

Something That Helped You Today:

_____

_____

_____

3 Good Things about today:
① _____
② _____
③ _____

Write/Draw/Doodle About Your Day!

Write About Your Day Or Anything You Want!

_____

_____

_____

Goals or Aims For Tomorrow?

_____

_____

_____

Date ....

Today I mostly feel........ (Circle One)

Or Draw → ( ) your own emoji!

How Have You Been Feeling?

_____

_____

_____

Something That Helped You Today:

_____

_____

_____

3 Good Things about today:

① _____

② _____

③ _____

Write/Draw/Doodle About Your Day!

Write About Your Day Or Anything You Want!

_____

_____

_____

Goals or Aims For Tomorrow?

_____

_____

_____

Date ....
Today I mostly feel....... (Circle One)

Or Draw ( ) your own emoji!

How Have You Been Feeling?

_____

_____

_____

Something That Helped You Today:

_____

_____

_____

3 Good Things about today:

① _____

② _____

③ _____

Write/Draw/Doodle About Your Day!

Write About Your Day Or Anything You Want!

_____

_____

_____

Goals or Aims For Tomorrow?

_____

_____

_____

Date ....
Today I mostly feel....... (Circle One)

Or Draw ( ) your own emoji!

How Have You Been Feeling?

_____

_____

_____

Something That Helped You Today:

_____

_____

_____

3 Good Things about today:

① _____

② _____

③ _____

Write/Draw/Doodle About Your Day!

Write About Your Day Or Anything You Want!

_____

_____

_____

Goals or Aims For Tomorrow?

_____

_____

_____

Date ....
Today I mostly feel...... (Circle One)

Or Draw ( ) your own emoji!

How Have You Been Feeling?

_____

_____

_____

Something That Helped You Today:

_____

_____

_____

3 Good Things about today:

① _____

② _____

③ _____

Write/Draw/Doodle About Your Day!

Write About Your Day Or Anything You Want!

_____

_____

_____

Goals or Aims For Tomorrow?

_____

_____

_____

Date ....

Today I mostly feel....... (Circle One)

Or Draw your own emoji!

How Have You Been Feeling?

_____

_____

_____

Something That Helped You Today:

_____

_____

_____

3 Good Things about today:

① _____

② _____

③ _____

Write/Draw/Doodle About Your Day!

Write About Your Day Or Anything You Want!

_____

_____

_____

Goals or Aims For Tomorrow?

_____

_____

_____

Date _____

Today I mostly feel_____ (Circle One)

Or Draw your own emoji!

How Have You Been Feeling?

_____

_____

_____

Something That Helped You Today:

_____

_____

_____

3 Good Things about today:

① _____

② _____

③ _____

Write/Draw/Doodle About Your Day!

Write About Your Day Or Anything You Want!

_____

_____

_____

Goals or Aims For Tomorrow?

_____

_____

_____

Date ....
Today I mostly feel....... (Circle One)

How Have You Been Feeling?

_____

_____

_____

Something That Helped You Today:

_____

_____

_____

Or Draw your own emoji!

3 Good Things about today:
① _____
② _____
③ _____

Write/Draw/Doodle About Your Day!

Write About Your Day Or Anything You Want!

_____

_____

_____

Goals or Aims For Tomorrow?

_____

_____

_____

Date ....

Today I mostly feel....... (Circle One)

Or Draw ( ) your own emoji!

How Have You Been Feeling?

_____

_____

_____

Something That Helped You Today:

_____

_____

_____

3 Good Things about today:

① _____

② _____

③ _____

Write/Draw/Doodle About Your Day!

Write About Your Day Or Anything You Want!

_____

_____

_____

Goals or Aims For Tomorrow?

_____

_____

_____

Date ....
Today I mostly feel...... (Circle One)

Or Draw ( ) your own emoji!

How Have You Been Feeling?

_____

_____

_____

Something That Helped You Today:

_____

_____

_____

3 Good Things about today:

① _____

② _____

③ _____

Write/Draw/Doodle About Your Day!

Write About Your Day Or Anything You Want!

_____

_____

_____

Goals or Aims For Tomorrow?

_____

_____

_____

Date ....

Today I mostly feel........ (Circle One)

Or Draw your own emoji!

How Have You Been Feeling?

_____

_____

_____

Something That Helped You Today:

_____

_____

_____

3 Good Things about today:

① _____

② _____

③ _____

Write/Draw/Doodle About Your Day!

Write About Your Day Or Anything You Want!

_____

_____

_____

Goals or Aims For Tomorrow?

_____

_____

_____

Date ....

Today I mostly feel....... (Circle One)

Or Draw ( ) your own emoji!

How Have You Been Feeling?

_____

_____

_____

Something That Helped You Today:

_____

_____

_____

3 Good Things about today:

① _____

② _____

③ _____

Write/Draw/Doodle About Your Day!

Write About Your Day Or Anything You Want!

_____

_____

_____

Goals or Aims For Tomorrow?

_____

_____

_____

Date ....

Today I mostly feel........ (Circle One)

Or Draw ( ) your own emoji!

How Have You Been Feeling?

_____

_____

_____

Something That Helped You Today:

_____

_____

_____

3 Good Things about today:

① _____

② _____

③ _____

Write/Draw/Doodle About Your Day!

Write About Your Day Or Anything You Want!

_____

_____

_____

_____

Goals or Aims For Tomorrow?

_____

_____

_____

Date ....
Today I mostly feel...... (Circle One)

Or Draw ( ) your own emoji!

How Have You Been Feeling?

_____

_____

_____

Something That Helped You Today:

_____

_____

_____

3 Good Things about today:

(1)_____

(2)_____

(3)_____

Write/Draw/Doodle About Your Day!

Write About Your Day Or Anything You Want!

_____

_____

_____

Goals or Aims For Tomorrow?

_____

_____

_____

Date ....
Today I mostly feel...... (Circle One)

Or Draw ( ) your own emoji!

How Have You Been Feeling?

_____

_____

_____

Something That Helped You Today:

_____

_____

_____

3 Good Things about today:

①_____

②_____

③_____

Write/Draw/Doodle About Your Day!

Write About Your Day Or Anything You Want!

_____

_____

_____

Goals or Aims For Tomorrow?

_____

_____

Date ....

Today I mostly feel...... (Circle One)

Or Draw ⟶ ◯ your own emoji!

How Have You Been Feeling?

_____

_____

_____

Something That Helped You Today:

_____

_____

_____

3 Good Things about today:

① _____

② _____

③ _____

Write/Draw/Doodle About Your Day!

Write About Your Day Or Anything You Want!

Goals or Aims For Tomorrow?

Date ....
Today I mostly feel........ (Circle One)

Or Draw ( ) your own emoji!

How Have You Been Feeling?

_____

_____

_____

Something That Helped You Today:

_____

_____

_____

3 Good Things about today:

① _____

② _____

③ _____

Write/Draw/Doodle About Your Day!

Write About Your Day Or Anything You Want!

_____

_____

_____

Goals or Aims For Tomorrow?

_____

_____

_____

Date ....
Today I mostly feel...... (Circle One)

Or Draw ( ) your own emoji!

How Have You Been Feeling?

_____

_____

_____

Something That Helped You Today:

_____

_____

_____

3 Good Things about today:

① _____

② _____

③ _____

Write/Draw/Doodle About Your Day!

Write About Your Day Or Anything You Want!

_____

_____

_____

Goals or Aims For Tomorrow?

_____

_____

_____

Date _____
Today I mostly feel_____ (Circle One)

Or Draw ( ) your own emoji!

How Have You Been Feeling?

_____
_____
_____

Something That Helped You Today:

_____
_____
_____

3 Good Things about today:

① _____

② _____

③ _____

Write/Draw/Doodle About Your Day!

Write About Your Day Or Anything You Want!

_____

_____

_____

Goals or Aims For Tomorrow?

_____

_____

_____

Date ....
Today I mostly feel........ (Circle One)

How Have You Been Feeling?

_____

_____

_____

Something That Helped You Today:

_____

_____

_____

Or Draw your own emoji!

3 Good Things about today:

1 _____

2 _____

3 _____

Write/Draw/Doodle About Your Day!

Write About Your Day Or Anything You Want!

_____

_____

_____

Goals or Aims For Tomorrow?

_____

_____

_____

Date ....
Today I mostly feel...... (Circle One)

Or Draw ( ) your own emoji!

How Have You Been Feeling?

_____

_____

_____

Something That Helped You Today:

_____

_____

_____

3 Good Things about today:

① _____

② _____

③ _____

Write/Draw/Doodle About Your Day!

Write About Your Day Or Anything You Want!

_____

_____

_____

Goals or Aims For Tomorrow?

_____

_____

_____

Date ....
Today I mostly feel...... (Circle One)

Or Draw ( ) your own emoji!

How Have You Been Feeling?

_____

_____

_____

Something That Helped You Today:

_____

_____

_____

3 Good Things about today:

① _____

② _____

③ _____

Write/Draw/Doodle About Your Day!

Write About Your Day Or Anything You Want!

_____

_____

_____

Goals or Aims For Tomorrow?

_____

_____

_____

Date ....
Today I mostly feel...... (Circle One)

How Have You Been Feeling?

_____

_____

_____

Something That Helped You Today:

_____

_____

_____

3 Good Things about today:

(1)_____

(2)_____

(3)_____

Write/Draw/Doodle About Your Day!

Write About Your Day Or Anything You Want!

_____

_____

_____

Goals or Aims For Tomorrow?

_____

_____

_____

Date ....
Today I mostly feel....... (Circle One)

Or Draw ( ) your own emoji!

How Have You Been Feeling?

_____

_____

_____

Something That Helped You Today:

_____

_____

_____

3 Good Things about today:

① _____

② _____

③ _____

Write/Draw/Doodle About Your Day!

Write About Your Day Or Anything You Want!

_____

_____

_____

Goals or Aims For Tomorrow?

_____

_____

_____

Date ....
Today I mostly feel........ (Circle One)

How Have You Been Feeling?

_____

_____

_____

Something That Helped You Today:

_____

_____

_____

3 Good Things about today:

① _____

② _____

③ _____

Write/Draw/Doodle About Your Day!

Write About Your Day Or Anything You Want!

_____

_____

_____

Goals or Aims For Tomorrow?

_____

_____

_____

Date ....
Today I mostly feel....... (Circle One)

Or Draw ( ) your own emoji!

How Have You Been Feeling?

_____

_____

_____

Something That Helped You Today:

_____

_____

_____

3 Good Things about today:

① _____

② _____

③ _____

Write/Draw/Doodle About Your Day!

Write About Your Day Or Anything You Want!

_____

_____

_____

Goals or Aims For Tomorrow?

_____

_____

_____

Date ....

Today I mostly feel........ (Circle One)

Or Draw ( ) your own emoji!

How Have You Been Feeling?

_____

_____

_____

Something That Helped You Today:

_____

_____

_____

3 Good Things about today:

① _____

② _____

③ _____

Write/Draw/Doodle About Your Day!

Write About Your Day Or Anything You Want!

_____

_____

_____

Goals or Aims For Tomorrow?

_____

_____

_____

Date ....
Today I mostly feel....... (Circle One)

Or Draw ( ) your own emoji!

How Have You Been Feeling?

_____

_____

_____

Something That Helped You Today:

_____

_____

_____

3 Good Things about today:

① _____

② _____

③ _____

Write/Draw/Doodle About Your Day!

Write About Your Day Or Anything You Want!

_____

_____

_____

Goals or Aims For Tomorrow?

_____

_____

_____

Date ....

Today I mostly feel......... (Circle One)

Or Draw ( ) your own emoji!

How Have You Been Feeling?

_____

_____

_____

Something That Helped You Today:

_____

_____

_____

3 Good Things about today:

① _____

② _____

③ _____

Write/Draw/Doodle About Your Day!

Write About Your Day Or Anything You Want!

_____

_____

_____

Goals or Aims For Tomorrow?

_____

_____

_____

Date ....

Today I mostly feel...... (Circle One)

Or Draw ◯ your own emoji!

How Have You Been Feeling?

_____

_____

_____

Something That Helped You Today:

_____

_____

_____

3 Good Things about today:

① _____

② _____

③ _____

Write/Draw/Doodle About Your Day!

Write About Your Day Or Anything You Want!

_____

_____

_____

Goals or Aims For Tomorrow?

_____

_____

_____

Date ....

Today I mostly feel....... (Circle One)

How Have You Been Feeling?

_____

_____

_____

Something That Helped You Today:

_____

_____

_____

3 Good Things about today:

① _____

② _____

③ _____

Write/Draw/Doodle About Your Day!

Write About Your Day Or Anything You Want!

_____

_____

_____

Goals or Aims For Tomorrow?

_____

_____

_____

Date ....
Today I mostly feel....... (Circle One)

Or Draw ( ) your own emoji!

How Have You Been Feeling?

_____

_____

_____

Something That Helped You Today:

_____

_____

_____

3 Good Things about today:

① _____

② _____

③ _____

Write/Draw/Doodle About Your Day!

Write About Your Day Or Anything You Want!

_____

_____

_____

Goals or Aims For Tomorrow?

_____

_____

_____

Date ....

Today I mostly feel....... (Circle One)

Or Draw ( ) your own emoji!

How Have You Been Feeling?

_____

_____

_____

Something That Helped You Today:

_____

_____

_____

3 Good Things about today:

① _____

② _____

③ _____

Write/Draw/Doodle About Your Day!

Write About Your Day Or Anything You Want!

_____

_____

_____

Goals or Aims For Tomorrow?

_____

_____

_____

Date ....
Today I mostly feel...... (Circle One)

Or Draw your own emoji!

How Have You Been Feeling?

_____

_____

_____

Something That Helped You Today:

_____

_____

_____

3 Good Things about today:

① _____

② _____

③ _____

Write/Draw/Doodle About Your Day!

Write About Your Day Or Anything You Want!

_____

_____

_____

Goals or Aims For Tomorrow?

_____

_____

_____

Date ....

Today I mostly feel........ (Circle One)

Or Draw ( ) your own emoji!

How Have You Been Feeling?

_____

_____

_____

Something That Helped You Today:

_____

_____

_____

3 Good Things about today:

①_____

②_____

③_____

Write/Draw/Doodle About Your Day!

Write About Your Day Or Anything You Want!

_____

_____

_____

Goals or Aims For Tomorrow?

_____

_____

_____

Date ....

Today I mostly feel....... (Circle One)

Or Draw 〇 your own emoji!

How Have You Been Feeling?
_____
_____
_____

Something That Helped You Today:

_____

_____

_____

3 Good Things about today:
① _____
② _____
③ _____

Write/Draw/Doodle About Your Day!

Write About Your Day Or Anything You Want!

_____

_____

_____

Goals or Aims For Tomorrow?

_____

_____

_____

Date _____
Today I mostly feel_____ (Circle One)

Or Draw ◯ your own emoji!

How Have You Been Feeling?

_____

_____

_____

Something That Helped You Today:

_____

_____

_____

3 Good Things about today:

① _____

② _____

③ _____

Write/Draw/Doodle About Your Day!

Write About Your Day Or Anything You Want!

_____

_____

_____

Goals or Aims For Tomorrow?

_____

_____

_____

Date ....
Today I mostly feel........ (Circle One)

Or Draw ( ) your own emoji!

How Have You Been Feeling?

_____

_____

_____

Something That Helped You Today:

_____

_____

_____

3 Good Things about today:

(1) _____

(2) _____

(3) _____

Write/Draw/Doodle About Your Day!

Write About Your Day Or Anything You Want!

_____

_____

_____

Goals or Aims For Tomorrow?

_____

_____

_____

Date ....
Today I mostly feel....... (Circle One)

Or Draw ( ) your own emoji!

How Have You Been Feeling?

_____

_____

_____

Something That Helped You Today:

_____

_____

_____

3 Good Things about today:

① _____

② _____

③ _____

Write/Draw/Doodle About Your Day!

Write About Your Day Or Anything You Want!

_____

_____

_____

Goals or Aims For Tomorrow?

_____

_____

_____

Date ....
Today I mostly feel...... (Circle One)

Or Draw ( ) your own emoji!

How Have You Been Feeling?

_____

_____

_____

Something That Helped You Today:

_____

_____

_____

3 Good Things about today:

① _____

② _____

③ _____

Write/Draw/Doodle About Your Day!

Write About Your Day Or Anything You Want!

_____

_____

_____

Goals or Aims For Tomorrow?

_____

_____

_____

Date ....
Today I mostly feel....... (Circle One)

Or Draw your own emoji!

How Have You Been Feeling?

_____

_____

_____

Something That Helped You Today:

_____

_____

_____

3 Good Things about today:

① _____

② _____

③ _____

Write/Draw/Doodle About Your Day!

Write About Your Day Or Anything You Want!

_____

_____

_____

Goals or Aims For Tomorrow?

_____

_____

_____

Date ....
Today I mostly feel....... (Circle One)

Or Draw your own emoji!

How Have You Been Feeling?

_____

_____

_____

Something That Helped You Today:

_____

_____

_____

3 Good Things about today:

① _____

② _____

③ _____

Write/Draw/Doodle About Your Day!

Write About Your Day Or Anything You Want!

_____

_____

_____

Goals or Aims For Tomorrow?

_____

_____

_____

Date ....
Today I mostly feel........ (Circle One)

Or Draw ◯ your own emoji!

How Have You Been Feeling?

_____

_____

_____

Something That Helped You Today:

_____

_____

_____

3 Good Things about today:

① _____

② _____

③ _____

Write/Draw/Doodle About Your Day!

Write About Your Day Or Anything You Want!

_____

_____

_____

Goals or Aims For Tomorrow?

_____

_____

_____

Date ....

Today I mostly feel....... (Circle One)

Or Draw ⟶ ◯ ⟵ your own emoji!

How Have You Been Feeling?

_____

_____

_____

Something That Helped You Today:

_____

_____

_____

3 Good Things about today:

① _____

② _____

③ _____

Write/Draw/Doodle About Your Day!

Write About Your Day Or Anything You Want!

_____

_____

_____

Goals or Aims For Tomorrow?

_____

_____

_____

Date ....

Today I mostly feel........ (Circle One)

Or Draw ( ) your own emoji!

How Have You Been Feeling?

_____

_____

_____

Something That Helped You Today:

_____

_____

_____

3 Good Things about today:

① _____

② _____

③ _____

Write/Draw/Doodle About Your Day!

Write About Your Day Or Anything You Want!

_____

_____

_____

Goals or Aims For Tomorrow?

_____

_____

_____

Date ....
Today I mostly feel...... (Circle One)

Or Draw ( ) your own emoji!

How Have You Been Feeling?

_____

_____

_____

Something That Helped You Today:

_____

_____

_____

3 Good Things about today:

① _____

② _____

③ _____

Write/Draw/Doodle About Your Day!

Write About Your Day Or Anything You Want!

_____

_____

_____

Goals or Aims For Tomorrow?

_____

_____

_____

Date ....

Today I mostly feel....... (Circle One)

Or Draw ( ) your own emoji!

How Have You Been Feeling?

_____

_____

_____

Something That Helped You Today:

_____

_____

_____

3 Good Things about today:

(1) _____

(2) _____

(3) _____

Write/Draw/Doodle About Your Day!

Write About Your Day Or Anything You Want!

_____

_____

_____

Goals or Aims For Tomorrow?

_____

_____

_____

Date ....

Today I mostly feel...... (Circle One)

Or Draw ( ) your own emoji!

How Have You Been Feeling?

_____

_____

_____

Something That Helped You Today:

_____

_____

_____

3 Good Things about today:

① _____

② _____

③ _____

Write/Draw/Doodle About Your Day!

Write About Your Day Or Anything You Want!

_____

_____

_____

Goals or Aims For Tomorrow?

_____

_____

_____

Printed in Great Britain
by Amazon

87090019R10068